THE THEME OF HAMLET.

"Thou art, too, like the spirit of Banquo."

A PAPER:

READ BEFORE THE FORTNIGHTLY CLUB OF ROCHESTER, N. Y.,

By Martin W. Cooke.

PRIVATELY PRINTED.

Copyright, 1887, by M. W. Cooke.

Charles Mann, Printer,
Rochester, N. Y.

In the interest of creating a more extensive selection of rare historical book reprints, we have chosen to reproduce this title even though it may possibly have occasional imperfections such as missing and blurred pages, missing text, poor pictures, markings, dark backgrounds and other reproduction issues beyond our control. Because this work is culturally important, we have made it available as a part of our commitment to protecting, preserving and promoting the world's literature. Thank you for your understanding.

INTRODUCTION.

It would seem to be the duty of one who proposes to discuss the theme of Hamlet, to begin with an apology. Every one who rises to speak in a debate which has continued for over one hundred years, ought humbly to crave the indulgence of his audience and preface his remarks with a declaration of his willingness to vote in favor of a motion for the previous question. This I do.

My confidence, in submitting these investigations, is inspired by the trust that my readers will be like-minded to a writer in *Blackwood's Magazine* who says: " We ask not for a picture of the whole landscape of the soul nor for a guide who shall point out all its wonders. But we are glad to listen to every one who has traveled through the kingdom of Shakespeare. Something interesting there must be in the humblest journal, and we turn with equal pleasure from the converse of those who have climbed over the magnificence of the highest mountains there, to the lowlier tales of less ambitious pilgrims who have sat on the green and sunny knoll beneath the whispering tree and by the music of the gentle rivulet."

I have not aspired to the rôle of painter, guide or mountain climber; nor, do I boast of sitting on the green and sunny knoll; but, in the effort to say an unsaid word of Hamlet, I admit a weakness which has led me to emulate the zeal of the young anatomist of to-day who burns his midnight oil in the seemingly hopeless task of discovering an unknown tissue of the human body; or, rather, the ambition of the mariner who refuses to profit by the failures of his predecessors and risks his reputation and his life in the effort to find, explore and reveal the fugitive northern pole. Furness says: "Upon no throne built by mortal hands has 'beat so fierce a light' as upon the airy fabric reared at Elsinore." I confess a loving labor with my little mallet and chisel with which I have busied leisure hours in pecking at this literary sphynx.

I would prove a peace-maker harmonizing the fierce contestants who have quarrelled over the problem. I would enlist for my cause and convert to my standard the champions of feigned insanity and of real insanity and their followers; and, allied with the smaller independent bands, I would storm this seemingly impregnable Castle of Hamlet, and let into it the light of day and open to view the dingy, ghostly rooms where mystery has reigned supreme for centuries.

Shakespeare pondered much upon the human mind. He created men with abnormal minds, and showed by their conduct, speech and tragic fates the personal, social and political ends of those who are "slaves of passion," and so demonstrated what the human mind is not or ought not to be. His greatest work was to show what the spirit of man is in this world.

In Hamlet he sought to reveal the thought that without and above man is a power which has relation to him and whose mandates constitute the law of his being. He postulated simply the fact of the supernatural and its relation to man. What that power is, whether the "unknown power" of the modern scientist or the revealed Creator; what its nature, other than that it is supernatural, he does not seek to impart. Man he represents as a being endowed with reason, will and subordinate spiritual forces—the passions. In this world man, so organized and constituted, begins his existence and tarries till death; and, while he tarries he is in anticipation of another or further existence beyond the grave. The end of man's creation is not here, and beyond the veil of death we know not what will be. He rests this part of the delineation with the fact simply that we will be—that there *is* "something after death." Here the state is one of struggle. We "look before and after," but our vision is limited by birth in one direction and death in the other. His purpose is to hold, as 'twere, the mirror up to the spiritual life of man in this world.

THE THEME OF HAMLET.

The play of Hamlet is the master-piece of the master-mind in literature. Its power to interest and entertain all men—the ignorant and the learned—is not possessed to the same degree by any other play of Shakespeare. The place it occupies in literature, its universal power to please, and the varied interpretations of it by the keenest critics, seem to justify renewed efforts to solve its mystery and discover its meaning and the secret of its power.

If one should read the criticisms of the play, with no other knowledge of the work, he would naturally infer that it was without meaning, and designed by its author as a literary puzzle. Did Shakespeare purposely create a purposeless production? Or, had he a consistent dramatic idea? Was he feigning insanity when he put forth this marvel of literature? Hamlet was one of the few plays that he re-wrote or revised. Shall we indict him for a second offense of fraud?

We have no sympathy with the suggestion that its author was merely a playwright, and wrote simply for ephemeral dramatic effect; or, that he aimed only at popular applause and the filling of his purse without regard to the meaning or worth of his productions. It is a libel against the intelligence of the playgoers of the time as well as an aspersion upon the author himself. Such a fling is the answer which not a few make to any effort to discover the theme of Hamlet. It is apparent from the work itself, and the study it has evoked, that it plunges deep into the mysteries of the life of man, not his political or social life, but his spiritual life;

and, if the interpretations which deal with it as a simple production, illustrating some one phase of man's being, have been so varied, so contradictory and unsatisfactory, is it not wise to look for a deeper meaning? It is fair to assume that Shakespeare had a definite theme before his mind, although Thomas Campbell says: "Shakespeare himself, had he even been as great a critic as a poet, could not have written a regular dissertation upon Hamlet." The true explanation, if it is ever discovered, will, doubtless, be consistent with *all* the facts of the delineation and, at the same time, account for the universal admiration and intense interest which the play commands with the people of every nation, for its power over the coarsest as well as the most delicate sensibilities, and for the diversity of the views as to its meaning.

Volumes have been written to demonstrate that Hamlet exhibits the vagaries of an insane person. Many contend that it represents the felicitous manoeuvers of a skillful artist feigning insanity to confound his associates. Others claim that it represents genuine madness, resulting from the effort to counterfeit the reality. One critic, in 1796, published a treatise on the play, and in his second edition apologized for the typographical errors of the first by asserting that it was published in haste for fear some other person would anticipate his discovery of the true intent and meaning of the author, and his theory was that the play was designed as an attack on Mary, Queen of Scots! This idea was revived and refined, in 1880, by a wiseacre in Germany. A German professor, in 1861, profoundly observed: "Protestantism will never fulfill its calling so long as its adherents are content to oppose the inexhaustible strength and cunning of its ancient evil foe with the mere consciousness of their righteous cause, so long as they will not learn to unite with the virtues of the Christian, the calm dispassionate prudence and consequent energy of the man;

so long as they continue to waste in foolish infatuation the power and aid which lie in their bosoms instead of using them." "This," he says, "is the end and aim of the lesson which Hamlet teaches." In 1881 a book was published in Philadelphia, the object of which was to show that Hamlet was a woman masquerading in male attire.

It is a noticeable fact that the members of the medical profession who have written upon this subject, for the most part, have claimed that Hamlet was intended to be represented as actually insane. The most prominent adherents of this theory are: Dr. Ferriar (1813), Dr. Maginn (1836), Dr. Ray (1847), Dr. Kellogg of N. Y. (1860). Dr. Connolly, a distinguished physician of London, published the most celebrated discussion of the question in 1863. Cardinal Wiseman advocated the same theory, in 1865, and declared that this controversy may be said to have been brought to a close by Dr. Connolly.

On the other hand, the advocates of the theory of feigned insanity are more celebrated in letters and in Shakespearean criticism. I mention Robert S. Mackenzie (1780), Thomas Campbell (1818), Boswell (1821). Richard Grant White contended that Hamlet was perfectly sane and a man of very clear and quick intellectual perception. James Russell Lowell is of the same opinion. Dr. Stearns (1871) admits that the majority of readers of the present day believe Hamlet's madness was real, but confesses himself to be in the minority. There are many other advocates of either side of this question, and it is candidly stated by many that the problem is insoluble.

It is evident that this play was not designed as a representation of the life or experiences of any historical character; nor is it an historical representation of events which may have occurred. It is a dramatic poem. The problem is to discover its theme. It is a mirror held up to nature. What is the reflected image?

It is the mental conflict of humanity in this world. The struggle is that which is common to the race and is between spiritual forces within the mind. Hamlet is made to feign mental agitation, the purpose or end of which is neither to show madness nor the struggles of the hero with the palpable obstacles to his action; but, rather, the conflict between his will and his passions, and thereby to illustrate that struggle which, in the life of man in this world, is universal and ever active, which begins with his birth and ends only with his death. It is the spiritual tragedy of humanity—the struggle between the higher forces of the being and the lower. The forces in conflict are under law, and the final cause of the being and the struggles is not in this world. The spiritual ruler within the mind is reason; the will is its executive; the subordinate forces are the passions. The passions determine action by their control over the will and reason. The conflict is violent or tame as the forces vary in strength in different persons and in the same person at different times. The tendency of each passion is to determine the action of the being exclusively to its own gratification; and its abnormal activity brings it into conflict with every other passion which interferes with its dominance and with the will as directed by reason. The office of the will is to control and direct action; and, guided by reason, to regulate all the powers which influence it. The rational activity of the will in conformity with a perfect standard of conduct, be it moral, religious or political, and the discipline and control of the passions to secure such action, constitute the problem of morality, religion and society. The law, by obedience to which these ends are secured, is from without and is supernatural. It is the law of man's being, which his Creator enacted and enforces. The play of Hamlet reflects the internal or spiritual life of man in this world. It represents a being within whom a struggle or conflict is ever active from birth to death, between the forces that are a part of his nature, each of which is seeking to control and determine the action of the being. In other tragedies, Shakespeare exhibits individual men; in this one—man. In Othello, he intensifies the passion of jealousy, makes it ever uppermost and dominant, and represents the individual under the influences and temptations of the single passion, in his struggles with the obstacles to his action. In Macbeth, it is love of power, or ambition, which asserts authority and control within the man. In Romeo and Juliet we see how love intensified and in full control over every other passion and the will, breaks down the being. In every other tragedy the mind of the hero is abnormal, controlled by a single passion or a group of passions; and Shakespeare makes the conduct and the speech and the results show the effects of the sway of such rulers in the mind. In Hamlet he has concentrated all tragedies. Here every passion is an active, powerful rebel against the will which is made prominent, single and constant; and every passion is intensified, but no one is continuous or controlling to the neglect of others. In Othello, Macbeth and Romeo and Juliet, we have rapid, fierce and violent action; for in each the influence to action is single. In Hamlet the forces which determine action counteract and cripple each other; and, although the struggle is intense and violent within, inaction is the result.

Most of the Greek plays turned on the representation of man's will hopelessly struggling, in calamities, against Fate. Hamlet shows the will of the same being, in his worldly estate, hopelessly contending with unconquerable powers within him whose subordination is never reached in this world. The life of man, in this world, does not justify his creation. Nothing here to be attained can explain or account for man's existence. And this is an argument that the aim and explanation of this life and its struggles will be found only in the " undiscovered country, from whose bourne no traveler returns."

The play shows the being to be commanded by a supernatural power or will—a will not of this world. Man's will, so commanded, is opposed by contending passions which are as much a part of his nature as his will or his reason, and each is a spiritual motive power; so a warfare arises, and peace is compassed only by the arbiter—death. The scene in which the ghost of Hamlet's father imparts his dread command is the dawn, behind which is the unknown; and, with the silence when "cracked that noble heart," begins the night when dreaded dreams may come, the apprehension of which gives us pause in life. The Bible shows man as a being created pure but fallen, struggling hopelessly in sin, to eternal death—the Creator assuming his nature, overcoming sin, the enemy of man, and helping him to his eternal rescue. The Saviour was a man obedient to the will of his Father, he was tempted in all points like as we are—yet without sin. He was what man should be in this world. The moral conflict of humanity is grandly pictured by the apostle Paul, in the seventh chapter of Romans. Shakespeare, uninspired, looked into the mind of man, explored the recesses of the human heart; and, in this play, he reveals and illustrates its secrets. The theme of Hamlet is the internal life of the same being in this world. It reveals a warfare which does not manifest itself in clash of swords or roar of cannon, but which rages, never ceasing, till the dissolution of the soul and body—"the rest is silence."

To illustrate this struggle, Shakespeare creates a hero seemingly having the highest advantages; he is a prince; the certain choice of the people as successor to his father the king, then dead. Hamlet is young; of matchless mind and body; keen in intellect; fully equipped with learning, strength and skill; of marvelous insight;—his affections already centered on the beautiful and accomplished Ophelia, who reciprocates his attachment; and, withal, he is "proud, revengeful

The Theme of Hamlet.

and ambitious" as he himself confesses. Shakespeare imposes on this hero thus environed and thus equipped with intellect, strong passions and delicate sensibilities, a commission, supernaturally imparted to him, to the performance of which all else must be, and is, made subordinate. This demands that the entire mind and all the affections, desires and feelings—the whole nature of Hamlet—shall be guided by his reason and governed by his will, which are bent on executing the command. It puts into conflict with his will, so guided, every passion, the gratification of which is impeded by, or forbidden in, the execution of the commission to revenge his father's murder. He is not prompted and controlled by his own passion of revenge. It is a being seemingly prompted to action by the command of the will of another and that communicated supernaturally. The commission was not of extraordinary magnitude except that it was for Hamlet to perform it. It was seemingly a simple act for him to do, but the design was to make him appear to be hampered and retarded by the influences of his own feelings. The supreme determination to obey the command of his father's ghost was ever uppermost, but not unshaken by fear that he was deceived. His will was opposed, not by the difficulties of the act to be done, not by the physical obstacles in his way, nor by the calamities about him, but by the powers within him which refused to be controlled—at times, weakening his faith in the reality of the command of his father's ghost and retarding his action when his resolution was unshaken. It is not the strife to stab the king, nor the effort to revenge his father's murder which challenges and enchains our admiration and courts our study; it is the struggle of Hamlet's will with—something! To discover the nature and scope of this struggle is the object of our study.

Shakespeare sees in man a ruling spirit — reason, whose executive is the will and to which all other spiritual forces are, or should be, subordinate, and yet whose throne is not impregnable. Its subjects plot and struggle for the mastery. Any passion unregulated and unrestrained, would destroy the system. Limited and controlled in their normal spheres, they produce a harmony of contending powers which is nature's greatest product. This is no democracy. God made man in his own image. The destruction of the ruler is the destruction of all his subjects. This spiritual kingdom runs on in secret as a whirling world moves amidst unnumbered others of like structure and is likewise governed from without. Its history is a conflict in darkness, illumined only by the light of revelation or illustrated by the poet's pen. The poet of the Golden Age painted man viewed in his relations to his fellow-man. The golden poet of the Elizabethan age opens to our view the internal mental life of man in this world. Virgil paints the building. Shakespeare pictures the occupants and the scenes within. Hamlet is the vehicle of the poet's thought. The play is the thing by which he reveals to others what he has seen in this spiritual world.

I will refer to some of the criticisms of Hamlet and endeavor to show that the true interpretation of the play, if it is such as I have surmised, accounts for their variety; and glean from them, as from expert witnesses, proof they may furnish in support of this view. I can only indulge in a glance at them, for the criticisms which Germany alone has furnished would equip a library with books. By some the theme I suggest is hinted or so nearly stated that it may be claimed it is not inconsistent with their views. A little more than a hundred years ago, the great scholar Lessing brought to the attention of his countrymen the riches of Shakespeare; and, notably, the play of Hamlet took possession of the German mind. It amounted to nothing short of enthusiasm—enthusiasm which never waned. Furness says: "Given a printing-press on

German soil (and the printing-press is indigenous there) and, lo! an essay on Hamlet." The whole German mind seems to have been inoculated with the matter of Hamlet; and the disease always has been epidemic.

"And now remains that we find out the cause of this effect." That it is a marvelous tribute to Shakespeare's genius is patent in any view. The man who could so stir the depths of German intellect by any wand he might create, whether one of magic or poetic structure, needs no greater praise. Is it a cunning monster that has so agitated this intellectual sea? Or, is it a creature of such delicate and mysterious anatomy that its structure has been destroyed by every effort at dissection?

If this play is such a mirror as now suggested, and was designed and well calculated to reflect the spiritual struggles of man in this world, it would be natural to expect that he who looks into it with no pre-conception of its character, so that the reflected image pictured on the retina of his "mind's eye" is undistorted by a defective vision or imperfect medium, will see *himself* reflected; and, in his heart, the struggling prince will find a sympathy born of fellow-feeling. Herein is the secret of the universal interest in this play. The simple spectator finds a response to his own struggles. For such a view the play was designed. The critic's eye may find what he is looking for (as the believer in any creed may find seeming support to his doctrine in the Bible), but he may, at the same time, fall far short of Shakespeare's thought.

Again, assuming that this view is the true one, and that the play is a perfect work of art, it would naturally be expected that any one who looked into it with the pre-determination that it was designed to reflect the characteristics of an individual—a possible person—would see reflected, either his own conception of some character he imagines represented; or, discovering inconsistencies, he would judge the person or character supposed to be represented, to be insane; or, to be an impossible consistent character except upon the hypothesis that he is feigning madness.

Hudson, speaking of the diversity of opinions in regard to Hamlet, and admitting that there are facts in the delineation which, considered by themselves, would sustain any one of the varied views, but none of them reconcilable with *all* the facts taken together, says: "All agree in thinking of Hamlet as an actual person."

This supposition, that Hamlet is an actual person—a possible individual—concentrates the attention upon Hamlet or the individual, diverting it from what Hamlet is imitating or representing, to the person he is supposed to be. Whereas, Hamlet is a player, made to act and speak as a man would act and speak under the influence of mental agitation, to the end, not of exhibiting his powers of acting or himself, but, to the end of discovering the mental struggles which induce the speech and action. We look into his conduct and speech, or, rather the mental agitation they evidence, as into a mirror, and we see reflected the spiritual struggle then considered. His speech and action are the external indications—effects—of the internal conflict. He is imitating humanity and he is not the handiwork of one of "nature's journeymen, that imitates humanity abominably." Shakespeare would not have the spectator look at the instrument he employs, but "rather the necessary question of the play considered." He employs his hero, not to exhibit himself, but to reflect his thought. The idea that Hamlet is an actual person—a possible individual—and that Shakespeare designed to represent in Hamlet such a person, is inconsistent with this proposition. Hamlet is the poet's vehicle, his instrument, by which he makes known his own thoughts. He is not exhibiting Hamlet, but using him as a mirror. The fundamental error of the criticisms that we shall notice, and, in fact, of nearly all the dissertations on the play, is the assumption that this is the representation of an actual person or character. See how it strikes Taine, the poet critic of France: "You recognize in him a poet's soul, made not to act, but to dream; which is lost in contemplating the phantoms of its own creations; which sees the imaginary world too clearly to play a part in the real world; an artist whom evil chance has made a prince; whom worse chance has made an avenger of crime; and who, designed by nature for genius, is condemned by fortune to madness and unhappiness. Hamlet is Shakespeare, and at a close of a gallery of portraits which have all some features of his own, Shakespeare has painted himself in the most striking of them all."

The German poet Freiligrath, with inspiration kindled by his poetic contemplation of the Fatherland, its trials, fears, griefs and joys, its hopes and struggles, sees the fond object of his dreams and subject of his song, and so he sings: "Hamlet is Germany." The politician sees illustrated the conflict of parties. The German student sees the German half-professor. The theologian sees the struggle of Protestantism with Catholicism or the strife of sects. The common thinker demands of Garrick the restoration of the grave scene, for to him the image is defective, wanting the element of the vanity of life. The medical expert sees the working of a mind diseased, the abnormal action of an unbalanced and disordered intellect; the philosopher— the futility of his principles and tenets when they come to cope with life's practical problems.

Goethe says it is clear to his mind that Shakespeare sought to depict a great deed laid upon a soul unequal to the performance of it. He says: "In this view I find the piece composed throughout. Here is an oak tree planted in a costly vase which should have received into its bosom only lovely flowers. The roots spread out, the vase is shivered to pieces. A beautiful, pure, noble and most moral nature, without the strength of nerve which makes a hero, sinks beneath a burden which it can neither bear nor throw off; every duty is holy to him. How he turns, agonizes, advances and recoils, ever reminded, ever reminding himself, and, at last, almost loses his purpose from his thoughts, without ever again recovering his peace of mind."

Of the German theories we have given Goethe's first, although it is the most familiar, for it is the result of careful study by the author of Faust; and, as a model of criticism, it was, confessedly, the "wonder and despair" of such a man as Macaulay. Further, it shows with the context that Goethe regarded Hamlet as an actual person. He even speculated upon the early life of Hamlet before he went to Wittenberg. These windings, turnings, agonizings, advancings, recoilings and remindings are the effects of causes—the causes being the internal struggles of the mind—evidenced—nay, illustrated, by their results. The reality, intensity, and continuity of these mental struggles constitute the theme of the poem and they are manifested by the effects described by Goethe, which effects constitute the mirror. Goethe beautifully and accurately describes the mirror, but loses sight of the reflected image. The great deed to be done is the control and regulation of the passions. The soul upon which the deed is laid is the will guided by reason. The power which lays the deed upon this soul is supernatural.

Herder says: "This work contains reflections upon life, the dreams of youth, partly philosophical, partly melancholy, such as Shakespeare himself (rank and station put out of view) may have had. Every still soul loves to look into this calm sea in which is mirrored the universe of humanity, of time and eternity."

L. Boerne (1829) says: "Had a German written Hamlet I should not have wondered at the work. A German needs but a fair legible hand, he makes a copy of himself and Hamlet is done."

Edward Gans (1834) says: "If Shakespeare's Hamlet is to be characterized in a word, it is the tragedy of the nothingness of reflection, or, as even this phrase may be varied, it is the tragedy of the intellect."

Dr. Herman Ulrice (1839) says: "In Hamlet we behold the Christian struggling with the natural man and its demand for revenge in a tone rendered still louder and deeper by the hereditary prejudices of the Teutonic nations. * * * The mind of Hamlet * * * is throughout struggling to retain the mastery which the judgment ought invariably to hold over the will, shaping and guiding the whole course of life. * * * Whenever Hamlet does an act it is not upon the suggestion of his deliberate judgment, but hurried away by the heat of passion or by a momentary impulse."

Dr. G. G. Gervinus (1849) says: "We feel and see our own selves in him; and in love with our own deficiencies we have long seen only the bright side of this character," etc.

Dr. Edward Vahse (1854) says: "Hamlet is the drama that utters the most startling, the most touching, the saddest truths over this deep riddle, this fearful sphinx called life; a drama that reveals to us what a burden this life is when a profound sorrow has robbed it of all charm."

Herman Freiherr Von Friesen (1864) says: "Let us now in conclusion once more consider that however our weak words may attempt to elucidate the great mystery of these world-wide complications, we must nevertheless bow down before its depth and unfathomableness. What is here felt and wrought out and contemplated, the unconscious germ of it all dwells in the breast of universal humanity, and therefore the tragedy strikes with equal power the coarse strings of the least sensitive as well as the finer and more tender sympathies of the more susceptible."

Prof. Hebler (1864) says: "Hamlet is Germany in

a most indubitable sense, in that the German attempts at elucidating Hamlet are the contemporaneous history of the German mind in miniature."

"No-Philosopher" (1867) says: "It is not in Hamlet as in other pieces of Shakespeare's, the history of a single passion, the development of a few mental qualities, good or bad, that is set before us. In this drama Shakespeare sets himself a greater task—to make clear and intelligible from the whole structure of the piece a human soul in its totality, in its fluctuating action and in the finest vibrations by which the nerves are thrilled."

Herman Grimm (1875) says: "A complete contradiction has been embodied in Hamlet, and a perfect contradiction remains alike mysterious to the wise and to the foolish; so surely as it is proved that such was the intention, so surely will this tragedy, as a work of art, forever have its effect; and, by the will of the poet, appear a riddle."

Coleridge (1803) says: "I believe the character of Hamlet is to be traced to Shakespeare's deep and accurate science in mental philosophy. Indeed, that this character must have some connection with the common fundamental laws of our nature may be assumed from the fact that Hamlet has been the darling of every country in which the literature of England has been fostered."

Again (1812) Coleridge says: "Shakespeare intended to portray a person in whose view the external world and all its incidents and objects were comparatively dim and of no interest in themselves, and which began to interest only when they were reflected in the mirror of the mind."

William Hazlitt (1817) says: "It is *we* who are Hamlet."

Macaulay says of Shakespeare's works: "There man appears as he is, made of a crowd of passions, which contend for the mastery over him in turn,

* * for it is the constant manner of Shakespeare to represent the human mind as lying, not under the dominion of one despotic propensity, but under a mixed government, in which a hundred powers balance each other."

If it should be supposed that Shakespeare did not intend to represent in Hamlet a person, a real character; and, that Hamlet was a being of his own creation, created not for the purpose of exhibiting himself or some person, but, as it were, an actor, whose office it should be to manifest the thought of Shakespeare by the mental agitation revealed—*feigned*, in fact—by his speech and actions, the different views seemingly so discordant could be harmonized, accounted for, or refuted; and those who advocate Hamlet's insanity would appear in error; and the alleged insanity, either feigned or actual, no more established than the insanity of any player who interprets many parts in the same play. Every argument in favor of the theory of feigned insanity is an argument that Hamlet is an actor; for feigning is acting. If Boswell and Dr. Connolly should come upon a man rehearsing his part in some tragedy for the stage, and, ignorant of his identity and purpose, should stop to consider his mental status, Dr. Connolly might claim the man to be insane; and Boswell, admitting that his speech and action indicated insanity, might, with reasonable argument, claim the person to be feigning madness. The revelation that he is an actor rehearsing his part would clearly discover the error of both. They might then agree, readily enough, that the speech and action of the stranger were designed to show the struggle with the passion then made to appear uppermost in the mind of the actor.

The continuous power over Hamlet, under all circumstances, was the command or control from without stimulating the resolution—the will to revenge his father's death. The poet places him in different situations each calculated to stimulate opposition in his own mind to the execution of this constant resolve, and force the struggle with the passion thus for the time being made prominent and active. The speech and action of Hamlet are the effects produced by these struggles, and these effects are the vehicles of the poet's thought—his theme is reflected from their causes. So we must not regard him as a person, but as an actor called to play many parts in the same play and all the parts so combined as to present a view of the poet's thought, which was: the internal, spiritual struggle between the higher elements of man's nature and the lower—the constant and continuous state of man in this world. The warfare is principally in skirmishes and in sallies, but is constant, bitter and uncompromising. Hamlet is neither sane nor insane. He is an actor. Shakespeare created him and taught him how to act. He did not take a player and make of him a prince, but he took a prince and made of him an actor. The hero might truthfully say with Clarice in the play of Comedy and Tragedy: "I am everybody—I am nobody." He who best plays the part impersonates most accurately Shakespeare's player—Hamlet.

It must not be forgotten that we are speaking of a poet whose insight was little short of inspiration, and that we are treating of that work which was the result of his great care. He did not create this character to show his creative power, but to impart some idea of which this creation was the vehicle of communication. In other works he had clearly intensified and made constant as the ruling power in his hero a single passion or group of passions—in this one he seems to have reversed the method and made constant and predominant the will apparently under law, and represented it in conflict with all other spiritual forces of the being.

Cole, the painter, conceived the idea of putting on canvas his poetic thought called the Voyage of Life. He grouped together trees, rocks and clouds, hills and streams, and with his brush he told his thought. The attempt to show that such a combination is a copy from an actual scene in nature would be like the impossible one of showing that Shakespeare's character of Hamlet has a possible counterpart that matches all his moods.

This tragedy is a mirror held up to the internal or spiritual life of man in this world. The struggle it represents is between the will, guided by reason, and the passions, under law from without—supernatural; the conflict is universal, continuous, and ceases only when life is extinct; and the result of the struggles, or the end of man's existence, is in another sphere.

If I am right in the surmise as to the theme of this play, the play itself should bear out the theory. I will briefly examine it in this light.

In this view, the play should exhibit (1) the reality —the fact—of the supernatural and its control, the law which is above man's will; (2) the theatre of man's life in this world; (3) the reality of the forces within, their antagonism and their relation to the will; (4) the manifestations of such a struggle as we have indicated within the mind; and (5) the fruitless result of the struggle so far as this life is concerned.

In the first scene the reality of the supernatural is manifested. The whole atmosphere of the scene is charged with the supernatural. Every word and its appropriate action reveal it. The spectator's attention is first drawn to a mystery impending, indicated by the mental agitation of Bernardo. The apprehension of the appearance of the ghost is apparent at every step. Francisco is entirely ignorant of the ghost. Bernardo and Marcellus are officers who have seen it and believe in its reality. Horatio is the scholar and skeptic who refuses to believe upon the evidence of the officers. This scene is clearly designed to indicate the nature of the supernatural appearance and the effect of its appearance upon the minds of these characters; and, by the conversion and conviction of Horatio to emphasize its reality. It furnishes a clue for the interpretation of the entire play.

We will imagine Shakespeare's instructions to the players in the rehearsal of the first scene. Shakespeare played the part of the ghost, and we may presume that he saw to it that in the scene where he appeared the actors were required to "suit the action to the word, the word to the action." The curtain rising should reveal a representation of Elsinore; and upon the side, but well to the front, a platform before the castle. The stage lights should be turned low. Francisco should be upon the platform, walking back and forth. He is to act the part of a sentinel who has nearly completed an entirely uneventful night-watch. He should appear as a soldier thus employed, anxious only for relief from duty; and ignorant of any unnatural or exciting surroundings. The scenery should be so set that Bernardo may approach in the darkness unnoticed by Francisco, and not visible to him, but in the view of the audience. Bernardo, while approaching, and before he sees Francisco, apparently hearing footsteps, should stop, manifest his fear by his action; and, in an excited but suppressed voice, or loud whisper, should exclaim: "*Who's there?*" Francisco, whose attention is arrested by this strange challenge, should stop; and, in measured, natural tones, demand, as from an unseen and unknown person: "*Nay, answer* ME, *stand and unfold yourself.*" It should appear that neither can see the other, and the voice of Bernardo, as I have intimated, should be such as not to reveal his identity. Bernardo, on hearing the demand of the sentinel, and, appearing by his action to recognize that the apprehension which caused him unwittingly to disguise his voice was unwarranted, should deliver the password deliberately, as he now perceives that it was the step of the sentinel that had startled him, and he should say, in a natural tone of voice: "*Long live the King!*" Francisco, hearing his voice, in its natural tone, and, apparently inferring from it who it is that has spoken—the scene and his action making it appear that he cannot see him—should say, in tone either of inquiry or exclamation: "*Bernardo?*" Bernardo should promptly respond: "*He,*" and should immediately approach, in plain view of the sentinel he comes to relieve. The darkness, the occasion, the manifestation of fear and the excited, unnatural voice of Bernardo, the change of voice, the recognition from it and the inquiry to verify the supposition from the voice that it is Bernardo are intended to indicate to the spectator that there is something mysterious in the situation—a mystery evidenced by these circumstances and the action of Bernardo's mind. Francisco unwittingly throws a light upon the situation by his observation: "*You come most carefully upon your hour.*" Bernardo replies: "*'Tis now struck twelve; get thee to bed, Francisco.*" The strange action and speech of Bernardo, followed by this suggestion, his mind passing from a state of fear to a desire of haste for Francisco to leave him there alone, when he was just now startled by the sound of a footstep, indicate to the audience that there is a mystery, and that Francisco is not cognizant of it, nor interested in it. The state of Francisco's mind, in contrast with that of Bernardo, is shown by his remark in reply: "*For this relief, much thanks; 'tis bitter cold and I am sick at heart.*" The spectator perceives that he is not concerned about anything but his own comfort and condition, and that Bernardo's mind is agitated. Bernardo again reveals the state of his own mind by his inquiry: "*Have you had—quiet—guard?*" This should be delivered in a hesitating manner. Francisco's prompt answer "*Not a mouse stirring,*" apparently calms the fear of Bernardo and convinces him that Francisco has not seen the ghost, and so he follows with, "*Well, good night,*" —adding after a slight pause, and as if the result of his suddenly realizing the possibility of the reappearance of the ghost—"*If you do meet Horatio and Marcellus, the rivals of my watch, bid them make haste.*" The spectator thus far having seen the officer Bernardo approaching cautiously and startled by the sound of footsteps he naturally might have expected to hear, suddenly changing his tone and appearance, and the change, and the inquiries, answers and replies manifesting agitation in his *mind* different from what would be expected of an officer coming to relieve a sentinel in the ordinary routine of his duties—indicated by his conduct and excited inquiry: "*Who's there?*" and his change of voice and manner, and seeming haste to have Francisco retire, and his anxiety for the haste of the rivals of his watch—prepare the spectator for a revelation of something which is disturbing the thoughts of Bernardo, but which is unknown to Francisco. The agitation of Bernardo's mind is not apparent to Francisco, but it is to the audience, and the attention of the spectator is drawn to that. Thereupon Francisco should appear to be listening and should move away from Bernardo, while he observes: "*I think I hear them,*" and calls out. "*Stand, ho! Who is there?*" Horatio (apparently assuming that he and Marcellus are challenged by Bernardo—expecting them) should answer in a light and unconcerned manner: "*Friends to this ground.*" He would hardly thus answer the challenge of a sentinel he did not suppose was expecting him. Marcellus, who believes in the ghost and is conscious of its possible proximity, should, in solemn voice, add: "*And liegemen to the Dane.*" This interview should be remote from Bernardo and out of his sight and hearing (Bernardo's by-play should indicate that he does not hear), and the reply of Horatio and the remark of Marcellus should be made before they come near enough to discover that the challenging sentinel is not Bernardo. Horatio's reply should be in a tone and manner indicative of the absence of reverence, and the speech of Marcellus should be of such solemnity as might be expected of a person conscious of the probable presence of the ghost of the king. Marcellus, upon nearing Francisco, who says, "*Give you good-night,*" suddenly discovers that the challenge was not from Bernardo, and upon this he opens his speech with the exclamation, "*O,*" and says: "*O, farewell, honest soldier; who hath relieved you?*" He answers: "*Bernardo hath my place; give you good-night.*" Francisco has been informed of their coming; hence he allows them to approach him without giving the countersign. Marcellus is startled, discovering it is not Bernardo, and so he utters the exclamation "*O.*" Francisco then departs. The contrast between the state of Francisco's mind and that of Bernardo, should be maintained, as well as the contrast between the light-hearted, skeptical and merry state of Horatio's mind with the solemnity of that of Marcellus. Marcellus calls out for Bernardo, who should not be then in sight: "*Hilloa! Bernardo!*" and Bernardo again reveals his anxiety by an excited inquiry, and in the manner of a call to persons hidden from view by the darkness—"*Say, what, is Horatio there?*" Horatio should again discover his state of mind by the reply: "*A piece of him.*" Thereupon the three come within sight of each other and the anxious Bernardo says: "*Welcome, Horatio; welcome, good Marcellus.*" His demonstration of satisfaction in this speech should be in a manner to show the relief of *mind* which their presence gives him. It is already evident to the spectator that here is one mind excited, anxious and apprehensive, calmed and relieved by the presence of Horatio and Marcellus, and another light and flippant, and another solemn and reverential. That there is some mysterious occasion for this is apparent, and Horatio is ready with the inquiry:—the beginning of his inquiry "*What,*" indicating his inference from Bernardo's action in welcoming them, that

Bernardo had seen the ghost again—"*What, has this* THING *appeared again to-night?*" The reference to it as "this *thing*" and the manner of saying it manifest his unbelief. Bernardo answers: "*I have seen nothing.*" In the remainder of the scene the ghost appears and "harrows" Horatio with "fear and wonder," by its appearance, and converts his mind suddenly and effectually. While Horatio is giving what is intended by the author as a false explanation of the ghost, it reäppears and its incorporeal nature is demonstrated, and its majestical character confessed. The omission of any communication and the full conversion of Horatio, the scholar and skeptic, coupled with what has preceded, reveal and postulate the *reality*—the fact—of the supernatural in the attitude of power and with some relation to human beings, but what its relation is, is not declared. That is reserved for its appropriate place. It is something more than a fantasy. It is the spirit of the Majesty of Denmark—the *ruler* —appearing from another world. This scene furnishes the key to the interpretation of the play. It is a mirror constructed of mental agitation and action on the part of the actors, and, it reveals to the spectator the reality of the supernatural, spiritual ruler, a ruler with

"the front of Jove himself:
An eye like Mars, to threaten and command."

We have seen the walking spirit of the king, but he has no voice for Horatio or the officers. He hies him away at the crowing of the cock. His voice and command are for Hamlet.

The second scene reflects the natural world, the theatre of man's natural life. Here we have the false-hearted murderer feigning grief, usurping power and rule, now wedded with his "sometime sister," preparing for war; and the libertine, Laeretes, home from France, and longing for return to the scenes of revelry. These inspire Hamlet's commentary on the "weary, stale, flat and unprofitable uses of this world."

> " 'tis an unweeded garden
> That grows to seed; things rank and gross in nature,
> Possess it merely."

Then the poet introduces the hero and here he unveils his mind. He casts a light on the tumult of passions. The beautiful form is dignified and pleasing to the natural eye. It is not outward demonstration—

> "Nor windy suspiration of forced breath,
> No, nor the fruitful river in the eye,
> Nor the dejected 'haviour of the visage."

He has, as he says:

> "That *within* which passeth show."

The distracted mind, tossed and tortured by tumultuous passions, cries for deliverance. Grief, hatred, filial love, suspicion, reverence, ambition, fear, are shown in raging tumult tearing the heart and the mind of the melancholy prince, as yet unconscious of his father's spirit in arms. He longs for dissolution of his life and soliloquizes with pitiful agony:

> "O that this too, too solid flesh would melt,
> Thaw and dissolve itself into a dew!
> Or that the Everlasting had not fixed
> His canon 'gainst self-slaughter! O God! O God!

This is a picture of desolation and despair, and the only refuge for the distracted soul seems to be in dissolution and annihilation. These contending passions here introduced are the forces with which the poet intends to put the will in conflict. The mental agitation is further discovered in the interview with Horatio and Marcellus which follows the soliloquy.

The list is not yet complete. In the next scene the author introduces and gives special prominence to another and more powerful passion. He has placed in contrast the counterfeit sorrow of the king and queen with the genuine grief of the prince and he again employs the same art by putting the affections of a libertine into contrast with the pure and true love of Hamlet for Ophelia. It is of the passion of love so revealed in this scene that the author makes Polonius say:

> "Whose violent property fordoes itself,
> And leads the *will* to desperate undertakings
> As oft as any *passion* under heaven
> That does afflict our natures." —[Act ii; Sc. 2.

The glimpses we have already had of this matchless mirror have revealed to ns the *spirit* of the king and father in arms, then the theatre of man's life in this world which appears a world of falsehood, deceit, murder, lust and war—then the mind of the hero occupied by and filled with conflicting and tumultuous passions, and special importance given to the passion of love. These are the influences to action which are to cope with the executive power yet to be developed. The *will* of the hero must be stimulated and so governed that its conflict with the passions will be certain and constant.

Thereupon the ghost and Hamlet are brought together and a command is imparted to the hero, the execution of which he recognizes as involving the subordination of every passion and he is made to promise:

> "Yea, from the table of my memory
> I'll wipe away all trivial, fond records,
> All saws of books, all forms, all pressures past
> That youth and observation copied there;
> And thy *commandment* all *alone* shall live
> Within the book and volume of my brain,
> Unmixed with baser matter: Yes, by Heaven!"

This command is *law* to Hamlet. It is the expressed *will* of a higher being, and it immediately puts his own will, that must secure the execution of the mandate, into conflict with every passion which would seek to determine, direct or govern his action. It is not Hamlet's passion of revenge that is to rule his mind and determine his action, but it is the command of his father's spirit and to obey his father's will is his duty, and that duty, to him, is a holy one.

The situation is intended to force the contest of Hamlet's *will* with every obstacle in the way of the execution of the command. The obstacles, we have seen, are not the physical impediments to the killing of the king, but the forces within his own mind acting in opposition to his will.

Here ends the first act. In it we have seen, as we have already stated, the power without and above, the theatre of man's life and action, and the door thrown open revealing contending occupants whose natural ruler is the will; and the will made single by the command from without. The forces have been marshalled, the field selected and the contest should begin. Our author does not tarry. The struggle begins in the next act.

The chiefest passion of the hero is the first to challenge the supremacy of his will. The poet again indulges in his habit of putting in contrast the true with the false. He has given us the stern command of the ghost to Hamlet and the genuine spirit of filial reverence and obedience. He has given us in contrast the precepts of the sage Polonius to his son Laertes—precepts full of worldy wisdom. He now opens to our eyes the wayward life of Laertes and his life in France in disobedience and licentious living in the interview between Polonius and Reynaldo which opens the first scene of the second act—thus, in the same scene, contrasting the exhibition of obedience with disobedience and the illicit action of Laertes with what immediately follows—the revelation of the first great struggle between the will and the passion for Ophelia in the mind and heart of Hamlet. We are not shown Hamlet with Ophelia. Ophelia describes the pantomime enacted in her closet. We last saw him parting from his friend Horatio when he took upon himself the dread command. Now we hear of him from the lips of Ophelia. Alone, in her closet, he appeared before her.

> "Lord Hamlet,—with his doublet all unbraced;
> No hat upon his head; his stockings fouled,
> Ungartered and down-gyved to his ankle;
> Pale as his shirt; his knees knocking each other;
> And with a look so piteous in purport,
> As if he had been loosed out of hell
> To speak of horrors,—he comes before me."

She tells in impassioned language how he took her by the wrist and held her hand and she says:

> "He raised a sigh so piteous and profound
> As it did seem to shatter all his bulk
> And end his being: That done, he lets me go;"

This is the mirror which the author holds up to the spectator. What a struggle! He was torn and racked by his love for Ophelia. What a conflict must have been raging within him to have brought this refined "courtier's eye" to such a plight! His paleness and trembling knees and disturbed attire obtained before he came into the presence of his soul's affection. The passion of love was in conflict with his will and sought to change his purpose. This was not weakness of the will, its strength was giant-like to wrestle thus with such a love—the love of "more than forty-thousand brothers."

This view is confirmed rather than shaken by the explanation which the blundering Polonius makes that Hamlet is mad from the pangs of love repulsed. It would not be artistic for the poet to make one of his characters truthfully explain the conduct of the prince. Polonius, particularly, could not be allowed thus early to pluck out Hamlet's mystery, much less to publish it to the court. It would impeach the author of weakness to suppose that Polonius hit the mark in his interpretation of the situation for the information of the spectator who is well aware of what Polonius is made to appear most ignorant. The dumb-show described by Ophelia "was never enacted" except in the imagination of the poet. What is passing in the *mind* of Hamlet is made to appear the great concern of all about him.

The next scene shows the subterfuge first adopted by the king to learn as he says:

> "Whether aught, to us unknown, afflicts him thus,
> That, opened, lies within our remedy."

Guildenstern and Rosencrantz, being *impatiently* dismissed upon their mission, Polonius appears. The business of the State—the report of Volteman and Cornelius—is *hastily* dispatched that heed may be given to the prating report of the prime minister as to the cause of the mental distemper of the prince, and then follows the plot to "loose his daughter to him"—to confirm Polonius' views.

Polonius plies him to find out what is in the mind of Hamlet. Hamlet throws dust in his eyes by the use of words all wittily expressed, but they confirm Polonius' erroneous conviction that he is mad. The dialogue, so far from convicting Hamlet of insanity, evinces a wit that any sane man might envy. Of the interview with Guildenstern and Rosencrantz, which follows, the same is true. They seek to know his thoughts, but Hamlet forces their confession that they were sent for to this end. The spectator knows their purpose. They come apparently to learn that which is plain to him, but they fail. This whole scene till the players appear, points always to the central thought—the state, condition and action of the *mind* of Hamlet. The attention of the audience is always chained to the scenes *therein* enacted.

The players then appear. In the recitation of the speech in response to Hamlet's demand for a "passionate speech" we have the counterfeit of passion—Hamlet calls it a "dream of passion"—in contrast with the genuine struggle which we see in his own mind, which follows the departure of the players; and he makes it a text to denounce his own weakness and inaction. He is made to seem not to know his own malady, for he says to Guildenstern and Rosencrantz:

> "I have of late (but, wherefore, I know not) lost all my mirth."

Later on he says:
> "I do not know
> Why yet I live to say, this thing's to do;
> Sith I have cause, and will, and strength and means,
> To do't."

Withal he was then the victim of suspicion, and under its influence he plans the play to catch the conscience of the king.

In the next act we have the sololiquy commencing:
> "To be or not to be."

This is the first glimpse we get of the world beyond—"the undiscovered country." It is the ever recurring query; does death end all? No, "'tis a sleep where dreams may come." That insight which reads the thoughts of the king, his minister and the courtiers cannot pierce the veil of death. Whatever that "something after death" may be it has relation to the acts, omissions and struggles this side of the grave. The dread of it "puzzles the will." In the interview with Ophelia which follows the soliloquy, the revelation is made to Hamlet that the lovely, charming, pure and pious "Rose of May" has been contaminated by the murderer's arts and that she has been led to submit herself to be his willing tool—and so he warns her to fly from the contamination of this world and seek refuge from it—not by suicide but in a nunnery. His soliloquy had just revealed that death was not the refuge to be sought. The commentary is not on Ophelia but on her surroundings. In the dialogue with Horatio which follows the speech to the players, he sounds the praises

The Theme of Hamlet.

of his friend in terms which eloquently proclaim him a model man whose will and judgment reign peacefully over his passions; and so he says Horatio is the true ideal of manhood and concludes his encomium as follows:

> "Give me that man
> That is not *passion's slave*, and I will wear him
> In my heart's core, ay, in my heart of heart,
> As I do thee."

His next words are (I make them mine):

> "Something too much of this."

If we have thus far matched our theory with the play it is safe to trust Shakespeare's consistency in the remainder, and we will leave this branch of the inquiry, although it "tempts us sore" to note the praying king's remorse and Hamlet's failure to "do it pat," and the grave scene is attractive—telling us of the vanity of this life and pointing us to another world for the end of these distracting struggles, and we would note Hamlet's rebellious anger at the burial of Ophelia, which nearly dethrones his reason in seing temporary triumph. Open the play at random and upon every page the wit, the wisdom, the acts and speech, and even "the wild and whirling words" of Shakespeare's hero illustrate the theme as we have surmised it. The tragedy is not that which culminates in the death of a victim. It is a spiritual tragedy. All the principal characters die—but all by *accident*—all except the one who was not "passion's slave"—Horatio!

Nothing is plainer than that Shakespeare will not stoop to the explanation of his own thought. He cannot be convicted of conscious exposition of his own performances. He respects the intelligence of the spectators of his dramas; and so the critic who would catch the meaning of the play from the palpable expressions of it uttered by the characters themselves will surely go astray. He who listens to the open declarations of the "foolish, prating knave," and accepts them as evidence, will certainly be misled. Notwithstanding this, we must admit that, as the author makes the hero say:

"The players cannot keep counsel; they'll tell all,"

so we quote fearlessly from the play to support our view.

Hamlet to his father's ghost, in his mother's chamber and in her presence, says:

"Do you not come your tardy son to chide,
That, lapsed in time and *passion*, lets go by
The important acting of your dread command?"

Laertes tells more than he meant when he says to Ophelia, speaking of Hamlet: "*His will is not his own.*" Hamlet seconds him in:

"There's a divinity that shapes our ends, rough hew them how we will."

And what Hamlet did for his mother the author does for the spectator: he "sets you up a glass where you may see the inmost part of you." Shakespeare "speaks by the card" when he makes his hero utter:

"What is a man;
If his chief good, and market of his time,
Be but to sleep and feed? a beast, no more,
Sure, He that made us with such large discourse,
Looking before and after gave us not
That capability and god-like reason
To fust in us unused."

Ophelia's genuine madness is the triumph of a single passion over will or reason. We have the judgment of the king, who says of it:

"O! this is the poison of deep grief."

The clown tells Hamlet that the loss of his wits will not be seen in him in England—for there the men are as mad as he. This is irony which an English audience could not mistake, for otherwise the play of Hamlet would have shared the fate of the speech which he says "pleased not the million." If such a speech were enacted, and the audience understood the hero was insane, it would not have been acted in England, "or if it were, not above once."

In the play within the play, a dozen or sixteen lines of which were Hamlet's, we have some light. The play king says:

> "What to ourselves in passion we propose,
> The passion ending doth the purpose lose.
> The violence of either grief or joy
> Their own enactures with themselves destroy;
> Where joy most revels, grief doth most lament;
> Grief joys, joy grieves, on slender accident.
> This world is not for aye; nor 'tis not strange,
> That even our loves should with our fortunes change;
> For 'tis a question left us yet to prove,
> Whether love lead fortune, or else fortune love.
> * * * * *
> Our wills and fates do so contrary run,
> That our devices still are overthrown;
> Our thoughts are ours, their ends none of our own."

If Horatio ever did—as he was bidden by Hamlet to do—tell the story of the prince; or, if he ever reported him and his cause, cruel oblivion has swallowed and suppressed it. The efforts of Guildenstern to pluck out the heart of his mystery, futile then, have been emulated through the centuries. Yet Hamlet's hint that he was an instrument, has been unheeded, unless Dr. Johnson intended to express the thought when he wrote, "Hamlet is through the whole piece rather an instrument than an agent." He scorned the attempt to play upon him by the euphuistic courtier, but he yielded to the touch of the master-hand with rapture; and, so played upon by Shakespeare, he did discourse most excellent music—music that will enchant humanity till millenium.

"Would not this, sir," even without a "forest of feathers," or even if the rest of his fortunes should "turn Turk" with him, or without "two provincial roses" on his "razed shoes" get him "a fellowship in a cry of players, sir"? Yes, a whole share.

And now comes Fortenbras; let him, as Shakespeare makes him speak, answer this query. Horatio's proposition to place all the bodies high on a *stage* gives him the hint, and so he says:

> "Let four captains
> Bear *Hamlet*, like a soldier, to the *stage;*
> For he was likely, had he been put on,
> To have proved most royally."

Is not this Shakespeare's hint as to the mystery of Hamlet? The author was about concluding a play which was to be, and has been, the seeming puzzle of literature. He had made Hamlet the patron of players, nay, a companion familiar in speech and action. He had made him magnify the calling in open declaration, and publish his own familiarity with it by criticisms of the traveling players—and his own recitations from the play "which pleased not the million" elicited the praises of the prime minister. He had made him appear as a playwright and manager, and had made him teach the dramatic art in eloquent phrase; and, as to a master, the players listened to him—players recognized and lauded as the leaders of the dramatic stage. Shakespeare, himself an actor, could not withhold his benediction on his darling child as he took his leave of him, and so he hints through Fortenbras that Hamlet was a player—to have stated it plainly would have been an offense to royalty and, probably, would have imperilled the success of the work if it did not the life of the author.

Here is an actor within an actor, a play within a play, and a drama of the inner man.

Printed by Libri Plureos GmbH in Hamburg, Germany